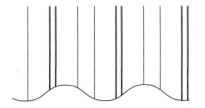

C000151332

OVER THE COUNTER

Life in a Rural Pharmacy
– and beyond

To Felicity

With love and best wishes

Margaret

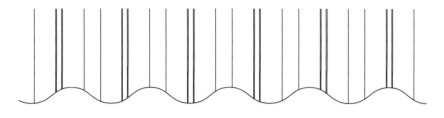

OVER THE COUNTER

Life in a Rural Pharmacy – and beyond

MARGARET ULYATT

First published in Great Britain in 2020 by
Bannister Publications Ltd
118 Saltergate, Chesterfield, Derbyshire S40 1NG
Copyright © 2020 by Margaret Ulyatt
The moral rights of the authors have been asserted.
ISBN: 978-1-909813-67-0
Cover illustration & design by Design Kabin ©
Typeset in Palatino
Printed and bound in Great Britain

CONTENTS

This book is dedicated to all my wonderful dogs down the years.
Bronte
Shelley
Shannon
Tessa
Leah
Holly

With thanks to my friend Wendy, for her help with copy checking and
sorting out the commas and full stops -
and to my husband, Barry, for pushing me along and encouraging me
to write this book.

INTRODUCTION
RELOCATION

April 1979. The end of what had been the worst winter for years and we were moving house. Not just round the corner or the next town, but over from Derbyshire to come and live in this windswept corner of the Pennines – Saddleworth.

"Where?" asked our friends at home. A good question. You wouldn't easily find it on a map as it's an area made up of several small villages delighting in such names as Delph, Diggle and Dobcross. We had chosen to live in the smallest and most remote of the villages - Denshaw.

We bought an old stone house dating back to around 1820, which, according to the estate agent, was *'in need of some renovation'*. Semi-derelict would have been more precise, but we liked the idea of a project and a challenge. We didn't know then just how much of a challenge it would turn out to be. If you started one job, you created three or four more.

My Mum was horrified. We had left a neat little semi just outside Chesterfield and she thought we were quite mad taking on so much work. She was probably right. We were making the move because my husband, Barry, had a new job in Manchester and it wasn't practical to stay where we were and for him to travel. So, we were on the move.

Dad thought the whole thing quite an adventure. I think he would have liked to have tackled something similar in his youth, so he enjoyed helping us with some of the many jobs to be done.

On the day our furniture arrived, snow was still clinging to the tops of the hills and behind the dry stone walls bordering the fields. It was early April but it felt more like January. The removal men wondered where on earth they had come to and couldn't wait to get back to civilisation. They'd had to come quite a long way round as some of the roads over the Pennines were still blocked with snow and the moors looked very bleak and barren.

Our furniture had been in storage in Sheffield for four months, so we were quite excited at seeing all our belongings again. Not that we could do much with them until all the work was done, we just moved from room to room and lived out of boxes for months unpacking whatever we could as we went along. Bronte, our yellow Labrador, was not impressed with all this upheaval. She never knew where her basket would be next.

The plumbers, builders and electricians eventually moved out and we began to create some sort of order out of the chaos, and Bronte found a permanent place for her basket.

I had worked as a dental nurse in Chesterfield and thought I would soon find a job when we moved, but there didn't seem to be anything when I started to look in earnest. In fact my first job here was playing the piano in the village school! I suppose living in the hills and not having my own transport, at the time, didn't help. Most places took at least two buses to get to, so when I heard that the local Pharmacy in Delph was looking for someone, I applied and got the job. I thought it would do while I carried on looking for a job with a dentist.

The rest, as they say, is history. I stayed for thirty-three years.

The following stories are a collection of memories about life in a rural pharmacy. No chronological order, just random tales from the Pharmacy in Delph and other areas of my life. Often funny, sometimes sad, we shared the lives of our customers. We got to know all about their children, their children's children, their dogs, their horses and their sheep. It is about the music and traditions which abound in this special corner of the Pennines and how lucky I have been to live and work here.

And it's about the wonderful dogs who have shared my life over the years.

They have been such a joy and privilege to own – or did they own me?

Also, remembering Billy horse. Such a character, if he'd been a little boy he would have had bits of string and conkers in his pockets and his socks would have been round his ankles. I rode him for seventeen years and we had some great gallops, sometimes scaring me half to death, but we had fun riding out with our friends, Jean on Rosa and Wendy on Bobby. Jean and Rosa would be up front, serenely cantering along. Billy and I would be next, rather less serene, my head on Billy's neck as I tried to avoid the overhanging branches. I hoped he could see where he was going as my eyes were tight shut. Then came Wendy on Bobby thundering behind us with cries of "I'm out of control!" Crazy, happy days.

1

THE PHARMACY

"Fifty parasols please" said the lady in the pink hat.

"That's a new one" I thought to myself as I reached for the paracetamol. In those days you could buy packets of fifty paracetamol over the counter. Not any more though, now the law has changed.

"Para – what did you say?" said our pharmacist, giving me a quizzical look as I asked him to check the sale.

"Sols – you know that well-known painkiller" I said waving the box at him.

"Thank you" said our pink hatted customer, "It's the OAPs' day out and we are just off to Scarborough on the coach, so I wanted to make sure I had some parasols to take with me, you never know when you might need them" and off she went. Not a lot you can say to that except "Enjoy your day".

With the senior citizens of the village on a day out, it would be quiet as most of the population in the village came into that category.

Just when we were enjoying a bit of peace, the door was flung open. Garden spades, forks, rakes all tumbled into the shop followed by an out of breath elderly gentleman. (Why wasn't he on the bus to Scarborough?) He carried more bags of tools and dumped these alongside the rest of the heap.

"It said in the local newsletter that you're a collecting point for unwanted garden equipment to send to Zambia. I've been clearing out the shed and here you are", he gasped.

He was right. The Rotary Club had put out an appeal for items and as our pharmacist was a member, we had been volunteered as a dropping-off point.

We thanked him and wondered just how many more rusty rakes and spades were going to arrive. We didn't have long to wait.

A wheelbarrow appeared in the shop doorway. We managed to stop it being wheeled into the shop, by the chap who had trundled it from his allotment just over the road, and found it was full of every tool you could imagine from spanners and hammers to rakes and hoes. We did our best and found some boxes to put everything in, but it was quite difficult persuading him that we couldn't take the wheelbarrow as well!

Luckily for us, the Rotary Club was very quick to collect the donated tools and send them on their way to Zambia where they would be very much appreciated. We have our uses – not always medicinal!

The rough moorland of the Saddleworth hills makes it impossible to grow crops up here, so we are mostly surrounded by sheep. Lambing time in early spring is a very busy time for our farmers, especially if things don't go according to plan and there are orphaned lambs needing special care. This is where we come in, making sure we have a good supply of feeding bottles and baby milk, and of course we have to have progress reports on our patients. It's lovely to see the lambs in the fields when they are old enough to be outside, and to think that perhaps we had a hand in making them such a delight to watch as they leap around or just doze in the sunshine.

FIRST ATTEMPT

During the 1980s, The Pharmaceutical Journal brought out another publication to run alongside the main publication, which was primarily for Pharmacists. This new magazine was aimed at people who worked in pharmacies and was full of practical information for all of us. They called it The Pharmacy Assistant and they were keen for pharmacy staff to write in telling of their own experiences of being in the front line of pharmacy.

I sent in an article about life in our village pharmacy. This was my first attempt at writing for publication and I wasn't at all sure what would happen – probably nothing at all!

I was thrilled to bits when the editor rang one day and said my article would be published in the next edition of The Pharmacy Assistant and would I like to write for the magazine on a regular basis. I wrote for the magazine for eleven years – the length of time it was published and I have the editor to thank for his encouragement and confidence that I could do it.

The following is the first article in its entirety. As you can see it's very short:

"Oh no, not the geese again! I'll be late for work if they don't get a move on". As I wait for the geese to cross the road, unhurriedly and cackling away to each other, I look up at the deep blue sky sitting on top of the hills surrounding the village and reflect how lucky I am that this is just about the only hazard I encounter on my daily journey to work, and how many people would gladly change places with me as they sit in traffic jams or race up and down motorways. The pharmacy is in the Saddleworth village of Delph, nestling in the foothills of the Pennines. In summer tourists seek us out, and along with the everyday round of prescriptions, advice and sales, the shop often becomes an information centre and sometimes a first aid centre. Tourists can make an awful mess of themselves when they fall down and they seem to get bitten or stung quite regularly.

In spring, sales of feeding bottles increase as the lambing season gets underway and orphaned lambs have to be helped along. When the snows come in the winter, sometimes the only way to get to work is to put your wellies on and walk – and hope the postman comes by in his Land Rover.

The joys of life in the country, but I wouldn't change anything – not even those geese!

So that's how it all started – and, as you will see as you read on, geese have a thing about me!

WHIT FRIDAY

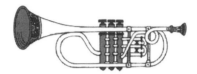

One of the great traditions of this area is Whit Friday. It's quite difficult to explain to anyone outside the area what exactly happens on that day. Basically, this is the day when literally hundreds of brass bands descend on our villages to take part in a unique open-air competition.

Whit Friday stands at the end of the week following Whit Sunday. During that week you can feel the atmosphere in the village change into an almost tangible build-up of excitement. New outfits are bought, best suits, probably not worn since last Whit Friday, are taken out and given an airing. It's a day when everyone has to look their best.

The main topic of conversation in the shop is usually about the weather. Will it be fine on Friday? It's strange, but somehow it usually manages to stay fine and sunny. We can have had gales, even snow, up to the day before, but on Whit Friday the sun shines on our Saddleworth hills.

Our window display at the pharmacy always creates a lot of interest. My Dad was a bandsman, playing the cornet, trombone and euphonium (not all at the same time!) and I used his cornet and some sheet music in the window and thought of the display as a small tribute to Dad. He loved Whit Friday and was very knowledgeable about the bands. It all added to that special Whit Friday atmosphere.

The village children acquire pea-shooters and black peas. They take great delight in aiming at random and, if you happen to get in the firing line, it can be very painful. No school for them, it's a local holiday.

As the village clock strikes 9.00am, our own brass band strikes up and marches through the village playing the local rousing anthem, 'Hail Smiling Morn'. Everything stops for them. Shopkeepers come to their doors to stand and watch the procession. The band marches over the old packhorse bridge which has seen many Whit Fridays, and back down the village street. Another Whit Friday has begun.

The village returns to normal for about an hour. People scurry in and out of the shops for provisions for barbeques and picnics later in the day. It's a great social occasion with people coming back to the area to renew old acquaintances on this special day.

Hymn singing led by the local churches is next. The band reappears to accompany the hymns and everyone joins in – shopkeepers, staff, and customers all joining in the singing. All this takes place just outside our pharmacy, and even though we are working, we join in as much as we can. It all makes for a very musical morning, especially with everyone in a jovial mood.

The afternoon is for the children with games and sports on the playing fields, then, as teatime approaches, people begin to gather in the village in anticipation of the evening ahead. Horseboxes arrive and beautifully groomed police horses are led out. They are a wonderful sight and so gentle with anyone who goes to talk to them and the sound of brass bands playing their hearts out doesn't faze them at all. We love to see them leading the bands into position to play in the evening contest. It's now time for the serious business of the day – the brass band contests.

For anyone who has even the remotest interest in brass band music, Saddleworth is the place to be on Whit Friday. It must all seem very odd if you haven't experienced it before and trying to explain it is a bit of a challenge. Here goes!

Brass Bands from all over the country and abroad arrive for the evening open-air contest. Sometimes there can be famous top bands alongside village bands, school bands, and bands just got together for the occasion, but all doing what they enjoy doing most and entertaining the very appreciative and knowledgeable crowd.

The idea is to play in as many villages as possible. The evening usually begins around 4.30pm and can go on until midnight. Coaches hurtle up and down our country lanes as they try to find the quickest route between villages. You never know just how many bands will play in any one venue, they just keep turning up, jumping off the coach clutching their instruments, marching into position, playing their chosen contest piece, and off again as quickly as possible. Chaotic – but it all seems to work smoothly thanks to the many people who organise the contest in each village. They do an amazing job and Whit Friday couldn't happen without them.

As one band leaves, the next one is lining up. The judges are secreted away in a building close by. They can't see the band and have no idea who is playing, they only know their number. When the band is in position, the conductor raises his baton and they are off with 'Ravenswood' or 'Knight Templar'.

As the evening draws to a close, dark by now, and the playing areas lit up, the crowds still stay to listen, not wanting to miss a moment of this special day. It's a long time until next year! Eventually the last band plays, the judges hand in the results, and the marks are added up and the winners declared in each village and overall. Tired bandsmen and women, sore-lipped and sore-footed, put away their instruments and go on their journey home, reflecting no doubt on the incredible day they have just had and already planning the following year.

Another Whit Friday has come to an end.

A FRIGHTENING EXPERIENCE

I t was a bright, cold January day. The sort of day to be out on the moors with the dogs, stopping every so often to admire the panorama of hills and valleys and tumbling streams stretched out below.

We'd had a very busy morning at the pharmacy with prescriptions and sales. It's amazing how the sun seems to bring everyone out.

We had just opened the shop after lunch and a few customers were standing chatting by the counter. Mrs. Sharpe couldn't decide what kind of cough she had, gave us a few demonstrations to see what we thought, and eventually settled on a cough mixture for a dry cough. As she paid for her bottle, she mumbled that a glass of hot whiskey was as good as anything and tasted much better.

Mr. Owen was in full flow telling us how much better his chilblains had been since using the cream we had recommended when he was last in, so we didn't take much notice of the young man who came in carrying something which could have been either a telescope, a fishing rod or even an umbrella.

It was, in fact, a gun.

The customers scattered in fright and disbelief as he came towards the counter, all except Mr. Owen who froze, rooted to the spot, chilblains forgotten.

Pointing the gun at me, the young man demanded morphine.

Now, this was all very surreal. I had known him since he was a young boy living in the village with his parents. What did he think he was doing?

Strangely, I didn't feel frightened. I couldn't believe this was happening and looked at him in amazement. I was able to usher the remaining customers out of the shop, including Mr. Owen, and as I pushed them out of the door, I managed to tell them to phone the police quickly.

By this time the gunman had made his way into the dispensary where the pharmacist was being forced into opening the controlled drugs cabinet. As his back was to me at that point, I managed to press the alarm button which I'd never done before. I wasn't even sure what happened when it was activated.

We gave him the drugs he demanded and he ran out of the shop. No heroics, it's not worth it.

When the police arrived, they were amazed that we were not only able to give them a full description, but his name and address as well. How did he think he could get away with it? Perhaps he was just so desperate that it never crossed his mind, but whatever his reasons, he ruined his life that day.

The police arrested him a short time after he had run out of the shop. We felt quite numb. Nothing like this had ever happened to us or any other shop in the village before, and it made us realise that nowhere is completely safe from someone who is so totally desperate for drugs.

The customers were wonderful. News travels fast in a small village and they came with flowers and chocolates and concern that we were all right. High drama indeed in our little village, but not the kind we want ever again.

It was hard to believe it had happened at all.

We knew it had though, when we overheard Mr. Owen the next day saying, "I was in the chemist just telling them about my chilblains, when a man came in with a gun........"

Life goes on.

HURRICANE TESSA

We knew, even before she came to live with us, that there was every chance she could be trouble, so when she arrived like a force ten gale, at least we were prepared – sort of.

Her Mum, Ria, was a beautiful dark blonde golden retriever who belonged to our friends Veronica and Trevor. They told us many times just what a character Ria was, so when it was announced that the patter of tiny paws was imminent, we quickly said we would like to have one of the puppies, a friend for our lovely Shannon. We didn't know then that a hurricane was about to descend on our otherwise peaceful household. Hurricane Tessa!

We already had Shannon, a beautiful pale cream retriever and so kind and gentle. She, too, was from our friends by their other goldie, Morgan, so we were keeping it in the family. Shannon, of course, was used to every possible comfort along with our undivided attention, but she was about to have her little world turned upside down.

When the puppies were five weeks old, we went along to decide which one to choose to come and share our lives. They wouldn't be able to leave their Mum for another five weeks but at least we would know which one was going to be our puppy. How on earth do you choose with eight golden bundles of fluff hurtling around? Well, you don't really, one would choose you, and there was no doubt from the beginning which one would be coming home with us in a few weeks time. She fixed us with an intense, intelligent and demanding gaze from beneath her enviably long blonde lashes. This was a look we would come to recognise so well, but of course we didn't know that then. We went to visit her each weekend until she was nine weeks old so that she would be used to us when the time came to take her home.

We took Shannon on holiday the week before Tessa was due to come to us. It would be her last as an only dog, and if she had known what was going to happen when we got home, she would probably have wanted to stay in Devon!

So, the day after we arrived home from holiday was puppy day. I was about to achieve an ambition – I had always wanted two dogs and it was about to happen, I was so excited. We took Shannon with us so that it wouldn't be too much of a shock meeting the new addition to our family. We couldn't have been more wrong, she was mortified and very cross with us.

It soon became evident that here we had one very confident puppy who was going to take charge of all of us from the word go. Everything was exciting. Life was a joy to be lived and explored to the full. Birds were a mystery. How can they get up in the air? Can I do that? She tried, landing in a heap and turning that disarming grin on us. Whatever she was doing, be it eating, sleeping, playing, causing havoc, she gave it 100%.

Shannon fell out with us in a big way. She wouldn't play with us, her toys and certainly not Tessa, and hoped every morning that she had been spirited away during the night. We tried so hard not to upset her, giving her extra cuddles and walks and time on her own. Then, suddenly, after about three weeks, there was a gradual change. Tessa was not a dog you could ignore. She was full-on with everything, and eventually, her irresistible charm won Shannon round and they began to play together. They became totally inseparable and quite a double act of fun.

Mealtimes were a very important part of Tessa's day. All her meals were tackled with great enthusiasm, but the highlight of her day was her breakfast boiled egg. She would pirouette around the kitchen on two legs, unable to contain her excitement. The dish would be licked sparkling clean, and when she was satisfied there wasn't a morsel left, she would look up, nose, ears, whiskers all covered in egg and grin that, by now, famous grin. "That was good – anymore?"

Her favourite thing to carry everywhere was a small green watering can in the shape of a frog. We would find it in her bed, on ours, in the car. We trod on it, tripped over it, she crashed it into our unsuspecting legs, and still it survived. Wherever the watering can was, Tessa wasn't far away.

As she grew and began to go for walks with Shannon, we noticed that nothing fazed her. She had no fear and took everything in her stride, just loving new adventures. Water became an obsession. After her first encounter, she decided that it was just the best thing ever and was completely focused on getting in as soon as she saw it. She could smell a stream, a river or even better the sea from a long way off and no amount of 'Tessa wait' could hold her back. Friends once joined us on holiday and couldn't believe the bouncing and barking from the back of the car as we neared the beach. Her enthusiasm rubbed off on Shannon and between them they created quite a racket. It got to be such an issue that we had to plan some water-free walks to save our sanity. I was terrified she would drown or be washed away. In fact, when she was in the sea we took to keeping her on a very long line, otherwise she would have just kept going, ending up heaven knows where.

She thought nothing of launching herself off rocks into the sea. Shouts of "No Tessa" were met with a sideways glance which said "You must be joking, there's water down there". Eventually we would fish her out of the water onto dry land. People on the beach cheered – only for her to wriggle free and run back in – "Fooled you". The beach cheered again. She caused much entertainment, not to mention embarrassment.

As much as she loved being in water, being bathed after a muddy walk was quite a different matter. Shannon would stand patiently offering one paw after another to be washed in the warm soapy water then dried on a big fluffy towel. Tessa's attitude was 'You'll have to catch me first' as she took off around the garden. She could kick the bowl of water over in seconds, usually soaking whoever had drawn the short straw to wash her. Then she had to be dried. We called her 'squirmy worm' as she ducked and dived out of the way. Every time was a major operation.

Shannon loved to come out riding with me. She would walk sedately by my side, obeying instructions to wait before we crossed the road onto the moorland track. "Over quickly" was her signal to cross over the road onto the moor. Then we would set off. Eyes so bright, ears back, she would look up as she ran alongside Billy and me. She was very obedient and trustworthy and Billy was very good with her, keeping his flying hooves out of her way. Sadly, they are both no longer with us, but what wonderful times we had together. Being out on the open moor with dog and horse was my idea of heaven, and I thought it would be even more exciting with two dogs. So, when Tessa was old enough I gave it a try. She was used to being around horses from an early age so she wasn't frightened – quite the reverse in fact. Trying to get her to run alongside with Shannon, who was doing her best to show her what to do, was something of a challenge. Never mind all this running at the side, she wanted to sit in the saddle with me, up there was a much better option. She tried hard to get up there and I was worried that Billy would tread on her. He was so used to Shannon being good that this new arrangement was a bit of a mystery to him. So I eventually gave up the two dogs and a horse idea.

Luckily, all our dogs have enjoyed travelling around with us in the car. So many people have told me that their dog just doesn't like being in the car and I usually ask if they take their dog for a ride whenever possible so that they associate it with a pleasant experience. It's amazing how often people say they just take their dog to the Vet in the car and not really at any other time. Would you be happy if the only time you went in the car was to go to the Doctor? They don't forget!

Tessa very soon decided that the only place to sit in the car was the front passenger seat. She liked to see where we were going and make sure the car was being driven correctly. She had a very keen ear for engine sound and, if you were ever so slightly in the wrong gear, she would look down at the gear stick, and then up at whoever was driving. 'Don't you think you should change gear?' And you did.

Being so energetic and doing everything at top speed meant she was rather accident-prone in her early years. Nothing major, thank goodness, but cut paws, and pulled ligaments were not unusual. Her timing was pretty good and she often managed to have a mishap just before we were due to go on holiday. Our dogs always come with us on holiday, so sometimes our walks were shorter than planned. Nothing stopped her though, bandages, lampshade collars, instructions not to walk her far, she was still determined to enjoy herself, and she just careered along.

Shannon and Tessa, what a team. After Shannon's initial reluctance to accept Tessa, they became very close and were just so good together. A whistle or call would have them turning as one and racing back to find out the next exciting thing – usually a biscuit. If Tessa had been up to mischief while we were out, Shannon would rush to get to us first making it clear that 'She did it, not me'. As if Shannon would. I don't think she put a paw wrong in all her twelve years with us. She was obviously the calm before the storm!

We learnt very quickly never to sit with a cup of tea or coffee in our hands or, worse still, a glass of red wine. Tessa liked contact and one of her favourite ways of making sure you noticed her was to nudge your elbow. After a few mopping up sessions, we got wise to her and didn't give her the chance to cover us and the carpet with whatever we were drinking. Not so when we had visitors. Many were the times we had to mop up a shirt or pair of trousers, apologising profusely, Tessa grinning in the background, knowing exactly what she'd done.

Sitting in the window, watching the world go by was a favourite pastime. She could hop up via the arm of a nearby chair and would stretch out full length along the window sill. Vases of flowers, plants and ornaments became a thing of the past. This was Tessa's window. At first, we just let her lie on the wooden sill then we took pity on her and put a towel in for her to lie on. This moved about a bit too much, so a piece of carpet was found which matched the one in the room and this was far more to her liking. When we had a new carpet, Tessa did too. Coming home from an evening out, there she was in the window watching for us. It was a bit like coming in late when we were teenagers, and for all the world she could have been saying "What time do you call this?" We always felt very guilty.

When Tessa was seven, our beautiful, gentle Shannon died. She was twelve years old. We were all heartbroken. Tessa had never known life without Shannon and couldn't understand why she wasn't there. She looked for her in the house and when we were out walking, but sad that we all were, it was Tessa who helped us through that awful time, which only people who have lost a beloved pet can understand. We had to keep going and doing all the same things and it was such a help and comfort to have her.

We needed another dog for us and for Tessa, so a few weeks later we went to see a golden retriever puppy. She was fourteen weeks old, older than the other puppies we'd had. The people were going to keep her for themselves after the rest of the litter had gone to their new homes.

Needless to say, we immediately fell in love with her and we were able have her and bring her home to Tessa. We called her Leah. Tessa took to her straight away and they were soon the best of friends and we felt we were a complete unit again. The strange thing was, when we checked Leah's pedigree, we found that she was a direct descendant of Shannon and was in fact her great niece. We felt so lucky to still have part of Shannon with us. Leah is so like her and she has her serenity and placidness– except when she wants something – then she becomes very vocal!

Leah adored Tessa. They made us laugh so much and we couldn't believe that Tessa was suddenly the older dog and not our puppy anymore, but she still lived life on the edge and she never really grew up.

The years rolled on as they do. Each day was a new adventure when she could have as much fun as possible and we couldn't imagine a time when she wouldn't be with us.

They say that no matter how many dogs you have had and loved, there is always one dog who will steal your heart. Tessa stole mine, we understood each other completely. She was still enjoying life at fourteen years old, going on holiday with us and swimming in the sea, but doing shorter walks. She began to slow down in her fifteenth year, but still had that sparkle which made her so special.

Just a few weeks before her sixteenth birthday we knew that she couldn't stay with us much longer and she made it clear that it was her time to sleep peacefully. So on a cold January day with Leah and us by her side, she went to sleep and part of me went with her. Our hearts were broken, but we were so grateful to have had the privilege and enormous pleasure of her in our lives. There was only one Tessa.

6

COMMUNITY SERVICE

The instructions were to turn right at the yellow cartwheel. I drove along the lane looking for the turning, admiring the sweeping views over the village and hoping that this prescription delivery wouldn't take long.

I could really have done without this on my way home from work. I would be late with tea and more importantly, Shannon, our golden retriever, would be late having her tea – her internal clock would be ticking!

Eventually, the cartwheel appeared at the side of the road and I turned down a rough track, wondering if my car would survive.

The stone cottage stood by itself at the end of the track. There was no sign of anyone around as I thankfully came to a stop after my bumpy ride. Just as I stepped out of the car, the door opened and two black and white collies came hurtling towards me. An elderly lady appeared in the doorway wrapped in her dressing gown.

With the dogs jumping around me, I made my way down the path and handed over the prescription. She was so pleased to see me, and I stayed chatting to her and the dogs for a while. Suddenly it didn't seem to matter that I would be a little late home. Despite my protests, she gave me a bar of chocolate. I felt about twelve.

Driving back up the track, I gave myself a telling off. Apart from the Doctor who had been to see her that morning, I was probably the only person she had seen that day, if not for a few days. It doesn't cost anything to give a little bit of our busy lives to make someone's life easier.

Thank goodness she had the dogs for company.

7

WHERE IS SADDLEWORTH?

I f you were to look for a place called Saddleworth on a map, you probably wouldn't be able to find it. It isn't just one village or town, but an area made up of several villages delighting in such names as Delph, Diggle and Dobcross. Nothing much changes here and day to day life goes on regardless of world events. Except, that is, for the Festival of the Arts which takes place here every four years.

For many months beforehand, feverish preparations go on as concerts, flower festivals, afternoon teas are organised. People are asked to turn out their attics and look for old photographs and any other relics which could contribute to an exhibition of 'Bygone Days', and in an area with such a rich history, there is never any shortage of material.

Drama groups and choirs rehearse madly so that their performance will be 'all right on the night'. Local artists produce new works to exhibit in various places around the villages and plans are made for many outdoor activities in the hope that our variable weather will behave itself for once.

As well as all this local talent, we are extremely lucky to have many internationally known people who come to perform at the festival, from opera and orchestral to jazz and rock bands, talks on gardening and mountaineering by well-known radio and television presenters.

It's a very busy week.

A spectacular firework display is held on the final Saturday evening along with a barbeque organised by the local Round Table. Brass bands from the surrounding villages play in the park and another special Saddleworth event comes to an end.

During recent years, times have changed and instead of our four-yearly Arts Festival, we now have an annual Summer Music Festival, which continues to attract talented singers and musicians from far and wide.

8

MAKING MUSIC

"Rubbish" yelled the producer from halfway down the hall. "You were all just dreadful".

We shuffled our feet and studied the floor of the stage. It was dress rehearsal at the local operatic society, and things were not going well. In fact, just about everything that could possibly go wrong had done.

It had all started a few days before when the costumes arrived from the theatrical hire shop. They were completely wrong and had to be sent back, and then when the second batch arrived, although they were the right ones, most of them didn't fit. Before any of us could wear them for the production there was much taking in and letting out of seams and waistbands to be done.

Eventually, everything was sorted out and we all had the appropriate costumes – only to find the orchestra in chaos. Someone had very kindly locked their music scores away in a cupboard for safe-keeping! More time was lost while person and key were located and the orchestra could strike up with the overture. So, all in all, we didn't get off to a very good start and it was the night before Opening Night. Well, they do say 'Bad Dress Rehearsal, Good Show', we could only hope so.

Basically, we were all tired. Even though we all enjoy rehearsals and have a lot of fun, the preparation for show week can be quite exhausting when we are fitting it around work and everything else. There are 101 things to think about, not just costumes and music and remembering your lines, but also ticket sales and interval drinks. The stage manager gets fraught with the stage staff when scenery and props are being finished at the eleventh hour. The conductor gets cross with the cast for not watching the beat, while the cast blames the orchestra for playing either too slow, too fast or too loud, and the producer just becomes more and more annoyed with everybody. And we call this enjoying ourselves!

By the time the opening night arrives, it's amazing that anyone is speaking to anyone else, but somehow we all stay friends. The surge of adrenalin and the buzz of excitement - not to mention nerves - overtakes everything else.

I've been involved with choirs and amateur operatic productions for many years now, and have noticed that they all seem to have one thing in common. Throughout the four or five months we spend rehearsing we are usually the healthiest group of people you can find. We manage to avoid flu epidemics, colds, chest infections and any other bug which might be around, but come the week of the show, we are suddenly struck down with every germ that can possibly attack our vocal cords and nasal passages. This time someone even managed to break an ankle!

Barry, my husband, says it's psychological. He could be right, but nevertheless it happens, and as I worked in a pharmacy I often got orders for throat pastilles, cough medicine and gargles, and would arrive each night like a mobile pharmacy. So I had my uses and it was all good for trade at the shop.

The pharmacy also became something of a booking office,

and it wasn't unusual to clip a couple of show tickets to a prescription bag. Just another service we provide at the village pharmacy.

After the disastrous dress rehearsal, the week of the show progressed very well with only a few minor hitches which were hopefully not obvious to the audience. Mishaps are usually noted and stored up by the rest of the cast, then given an airing at the aftershow party, which was just like putting on another show!

The final night arrived and everyone was in high spirits. We were all chatting and exchanging cards and presents in the dressing rooms when someone realised that the leading man was nowhere to be seen. It was getting dangerously close to curtain up and we had to decide what to do if he didn't arrive in time – or at all.

A 'volunteer' from the chorus was put on standby. He quickly changed into the lead's costume, which with the help of a few pins was made to fit him, then just as the orchestra struck up with the overture, the leading man burst in. He'd been stuck in a traffic jam caused by an accident. The chorus member then had to be unpinned and the lead set a world record for getting dressed. Never a dull moment right to the end.

What a week it had been – and the name of the show?

'Patience' by Gilbert and Sullivan.

We certainly needed some!

A HIGHLAND FLING

We were three days into our holiday in Scotland and it was still raining. So far nothing had endeared us to this supposedly beautiful part of our island home.

We had driven up in glorious sunshine. Not the best weather to spend seven hours in a car but we were so looking forward to our holiday and had lots of plans to walk through woods and on mountain paths. Shannon, our young retriever, would be able to run for miles, using up some of her boundless energy. Three days on and the chances of achieving any of our plans seemed more and more remote.

Our holiday cottage in the Highlands was, luckily, very warm and cosy so we could at least dry off in comfort. It was situated at the end of a track surrounded by deer and sheep, but because of the persistent low cloud over the mountains, the sky looked as though it was on the floor. We knew that somewhere out there were spectacular views and glorious scenery. We had yet to see it and hoped each night that the following day would be better.

The fourth morning dawned just the same, pouring rain and the sky was still on the floor. We were running out of dog towels for drying Shannon. You just have to go out with a dog whatever the weather and we had gone through what we thought was an ample supply in a couple of days.

At lunchtime that day, as we ate our picnic lunch yet again in the car, we began to notice a slight change in the relentless downpour. A lighter sound, a brightening in the gloom, and, at last, the sky began to resume its normal place. Gradually we could see hills and mountains, the clouds began to break up, and yes, a glimmer, a hint of what could just possibly be sunshine. Everywhere began to steam, but we didn't mind that, at last the rain had stopped. Things were looking up!

One of the plans we had talked about on our sunny journey north had been to go up Ben Nevis. The weather continued to improve, so the following morning saw us suitably equipped and ready to go. We'd had plenty of time during the previous wet days to read up on the preparation needed for what the guide books called 'A memorable climb. More people have been killed on Ben Nevis than on the north face of the Eiger' one book cheerfully told us. Do I really want to do this, I thought. Will Shannon be all right, will it be too much for her? (Will it be too much for me?) Barry was full of enthusiasm and couldn't wait to get started. He'd done quite a lot of climbing in his younger days and was raring to go. He had taken the list of essential items very seriously and we were prepared for any eventuality in any climate – Shannon too! Captain Scott would have been proud of us. I usually just carried the dog lead, but for this excursion I had a rucksack to carry as well.

As we started to climb, it was obvious that lots more people had been waiting for the weather to improve, and there was quite a party atmosphere as we all set off. Shannon, of course, made many friends along the way. Few people could resist her charms, and she was at her most beguiling if you just happened to be munching a packet of crisps. She was very adaptable and had often had her lunch in the strangest of places – car parks, middle of fields, and the backseat of the car – so even if you are halfway up a mountain, lunchtime is lunchtime. We perched thankfully on a convenient rock to admire the view and eat our picnic while she happily tucked into her lunch, causing much amusement amongst our fellow climbers.

We were getting quite high now and houses, cars and people were just little dots below us. The full panorama of the glen below and the majestic mountain above us was beginning to unfold. It quite took our breath away. The weather was just right, very clear and not too warm. We could actually see the summit above and it looked an awfully long way off! This was scenery on a grand scale and, as it's something you probably only do once, you just have to stop and drink it all in.

As we neared the top, we could feel the temperature drop considerably and we were soon walking through snow. Shannon was in her element, she loved snow. We put on extra layers of clothes – less to carry in the rucksack.

Sadly, just as we walked the last few feet to the very top, we became enveloped in cloud and the spectacular views disappeared. The ruins of an observatory and a hotel (hotel, up there?), combined with the cairn commemorating war casualties, all seemed very spooky in the swirling mist. Everyone moved very quietly between the barren rocks, like spectres in the gloom, but it was an amazing, invigorating feeling being right up there at the very top. We had made it, Shannon too, all 4,406 feet of it and we all felt very proud of ourselves.

We had another picnic, this time in snow, and took lots of photographs. Shannon managed to get herself photographed and filmed by people from far-flung corners of the world and would have appeared in home movies in Australia, Japan and Germany. Remembering that the guide book told us not to linger too long at the top, as it's still a long way back down, we soon began our descent. Going down needed just as much care as the climb up. Apparently, most accidents happen when people are tired and not concentrating. We emerged from the mist and played with Shannon in the snow, making sure we didn't go near the edge – we didn't fancy the quick route down.

The weather cleared as we began our descent and we were able to appreciate the incredible landscape before us. It is a very tiring, arduous climb and the eventual sight of the car park below was very welcome, although it did seem to take a long time to get there.

The whole trek had taken eight hours, a climb of twelve miles with an ascent of 4,406 feet. It had been a daunting prospect as we set off that morning, but now we had actually completed it, we felt very pleased with ourselves and Shannon. She had been such a good girl, no trouble at all, and had made a lot of friends. My feet ached, my knees felt as though they didn't belong to me and I just couldn't wait to get rid of that rucksack.

As soon as we arrived back at our cottage, Shannon had her tea then curled up in her basket and fell fast asleep, a contented, happy dog.

We did much the same.

Above: Home in winter – a challenge but well worth it.

Above: Where it all began - The Pharmacy in Delph.

Above: The geese who made me late for work.

Above & left: Whit Friday morning, the traditional Church Parade of Witness around the village.

Above: Whit Friday morning and the Delph Brass Band march into the village over the old packhorse bridge.

Left: Police horses waiting to lead the Whit Friday bands into position.

Below: Whit Friday evening, the serious business of the day – the Brass Band Contest.

Top and Above: Tessa,
12 weeks old and
growing up fast into the
'hurricane' she became.

Left: Tessa and her 'I'm in
water' pose – 'You'll have
to come and get me out!'

Above: Tessa and Leah in the snow.

Above: Treading the boards – with Saddleworth Musical Society.

Above: Ben Nevis – the summit. Well done Shannon.

Above: Interesting windows make all the difference.

Top: Saddleworth in winter.

Above: The geese 'Laurel and Hardy' looking for trouble.

Right: Uncle Silas at the Sabden Treacle Mines.

Above & left: Leah and Holly.

10

15 MINUTES OF FAME

It's often said that here in our windswept corner of the Pennines, we live a very sheltered existence which has nothing to do with the hills which surround the villages. We often don't take a lot of notice of what is happening elsewhere and tend to live in our own little world. The solid stone buildings and the old packhorse bridge over the river reflect a bygone age when time moved more slowly than it does today.

The village is full of characters that we get to know well, as most people need the services of the pharmacy at sometime, whether it's to collect a prescription or to buy a new toothbrush. As everyone knows each other in the village, the whole shop tends to have a conversation rather than just individuals. An elderly customer was once describing his stay in hospital in great detail to the assembled people in the shop. Suddenly, he rolled up his trouser leg to show off his newly fitted leg bag. I held my breath, wondering how the other customers would react. I needn't have worried; nobody batted an eyelid. They just inspected it, nodded sagely, then wished him well as he left the shop with his prescription. It occurred to me that there could have been a very different reaction if that had happened in a certain high street store not many miles away.

Sometimes, though, something happens which takes us out of our little bubble and catapults us right into the real world, whether we like it or not.

One day, a letter arrived at the pharmacy which caused great excitement. A film crew from the BBC was coming to the village to record an advert for a new programme. We were going to be famous!

This was the second time our village had been sought out for filming. If you have watched the film 'Brassed Off' you will have seen us on the big screen, when scenes from our Whit Friday band contests were used in the film. Quite a few local people were extras, and some even had speaking parts. Fame at last.

The film crew, their vehicles and equipment set up camp in the pub car park. It was as though another village had settled itself into the middle of ours. There seemed to be hundreds of people wandering around not doing anything very much. Some of them came into the shop for make-up and hair accessories, while others were in need of cough and cold relief supplies. We felt quite useful and part of what was happening. Our customers, on the other hand, seemed to be keeping out of the way, we didn't see many familiar faces.

It all seemed to take a very long time, and the village street had to be closed while they filmed a man on a bike chasing after a red car – lots of times!

We never did find out what it was all to do with, but it was fun while it lasted and we enjoyed our little bit of stardom.

11

LOCUMS

The phone rang just as I was about to set off on my lunchtime walk with Shelley, our golden retriever. She lay down and gave me a disgusted look as I went to answer it.

"I'm completely shattered" said the exhausted voice at the other end of the phone. "Good luck this afternoon, I'm worn out". This was Annie, our morning staff at the pharmacy and she had obviously had a hectic morning with a new locum who was with us while our boss was on holiday.

Unfortunately, you never know who you are going to get, and this particular locum had been retired from his own business for quite some time, so was somewhat out of touch with working in a busy up to date pharmacy. By the end of that fortnight we were worn out, and I'm sure he was too! But it must be difficult to just slot into a different routine in a different dispensary with different staff.

Delph is a moorland village surrounded by lovely countryside and the Saddleworth hills. We are very lucky to live and work here, and most of the locums find it a welcome change from High Street pharmacies in the middle of towns. They often take the opportunity to have a stroll around the village and have a breath of fresh air when the shop closes for lunch.

The graveyard just across the road from the shop was a particular favourite lunchtime walk for one of our locums. He was fascinated by ancient tombstones which go back hundreds of years, many bearing the same surnames as the customers we still dispensed prescriptions for. He liked nothing better than a cheerful discussion on deaths in the village down the centuries.

He also had a daily ritual of afternoon tea. Not just a quick cuppa grabbed between customers, but sandwiches as well. He had a real passion for spring onions, and every day, he set out his snack in the dispensary. We usually beat a hasty retreat into the shop, but should he have cause to come up and speak to a customer about their medication, you could see them take a couple of steps backwards as he breathed spring onion fumes over them – not the best thing for customer relations!

One of our regular locums had been qualified a long time and it was interesting to hear how pharmacy has changed over the years. Most preparations had to be made up in the dispensary – ointments, cough medicines, even suppositories, and all labels were handwritten. No computers then. Life was slower and people didn't mind waiting. It was a chance to have a chat with whoever else was there and put the world to rights.

Computers, in general, caused us a lot of hassle when we first used them. They seemed to have a mind of their own, especially when the boss was away and the locum hadn't got a clue what to do when things went wrong. Why did it print fifteen labels for Mrs. Smith's eye drops when we only wanted one? (Nothing to do, of course, with pressing the wrong key!) These strange things never seemed to happen when the boss was there.

So while he was enjoying the sun hundreds of miles away, we

just carried on and coped with locums, computers, reps., wailing children, queries and anything a typical day could throw at us.

"Everything all right?" he would ask when he came back.

"Oh fine" we would say.

12

A WELSH INTERLUDE

I t all started with a note on a Christmas card from friends who live in a remote farmhouse in Wales.

"How do you fancy house-sitting for us in August?"

Now, viewed from the fireside on a freezing cold day, with snow falling past the window, the thought of a sunny week in a beautiful old farmhouse set in the glorious Welsh countryside had a certain appeal. The reality was that the house-sitting included looking after a menagerie of two dogs (three when we arrived with Shannon), three cats, countless hens and cockerels and two geese who could be very tricky and liked to think they were in charge of everything and everybody.

The house itself, although in an enviable spot, was, as they say, "being done up".

We thought it would be a good idea to pay a visit beforehand if only to make sure that the dogs all got along together. It wouldn't be much fun if they took exception to each other and had to be kept apart all week. So on a very wet weekend in March, we drove down to see what we might be letting ourselves in for.

It poured with rain all the way, but we were sure it would all look so much better in blazing August sunshine, so we didn't worry too much about the mist and rain which obscured what would have been a spectacular view of the Welsh hills.

As we arrived, the dogs ran around each other, barking and generally weighing each other up but they soon settled down. First hurdle over. They would probably just ignore each other all the week we were there. Shannon likes the quiet life so she wouldn't look for trouble.

The elderly German Shepherd was a bit unsteady on her pins but very sweet and gentle, and the little mongrel of indeterminate parentage was a real character.

Our friends gave us a guided tour of their house and gardens. We soon realised that there was a lot of 'work in progress' going on but they assured it would all be finished by August, and the builders would have moved out. We hoped so.

The weeks flew by as they do and before we knew it we were packing to go. For two and a half weeks we had sizzled in a heat wave, and things looked promising for our holiday with a difference.

We planned to leave after work on the Friday and arrive early evening as our friends had a ferry to catch that night and we wanted to see them before they left. Shannon ran round in circles making sure she wasn't left behind – as if we would. As we packed the car, we noticed a subtle change in the weather. The sky darkened, there was a mighty crack of thunder and the heavens opened. We drove all the way in torrential rain and arrived at the farm in just the same weather as on our visit in March. It rained until Tuesday.

The builders had been hard at work on and mostly off for weeks. Now they had departed – about two hours before we arrived – leaving a major clearing up job to be done. Our friends were most embarrassed about the state of chaos which greeted us when we arrived, but they had a ferry to catch. There was nothing for it but to send them off, roll up our sleeves and get on with trying to clean up. Well, it was raining anyway, not fit to sit in the garden with a glass of wine as we'd hoped! We eventually restored some sort of order and opened that bottle of wine.

Animals don't care if it's raining or not, so, remembering why we were actually there, we got down to our chores – who said holiday?

We had the dogs to feed and walk, cats to feed, and didn't they let us know when their dishes were empty, ducks and hens to feed and eggs to collect.

And then there were the geese.

The geese were a double act, they did everything and went everywhere together and had a wicked sense of humour. Shannon learnt very quickly to keep out of their way and give them a wide berth if she heard them coming towards her. We christened them Laurel and Hardy which we thought suited them. They struck up a firm friendship with Barry and would walk alongside him cackling away, telling him such a tale. He said the secret was to be firm with them, don't let them get away with anything, and they would behave themselves.

That didn't seem to work for me. One of them whipped a towel out of my hand as I walked past and, on another occasion, had the toe of my welly in its beak. (Yes it was still raining). Each time I stepped outside I had to check where they were. It became quite a battle of wits to discover where they were lying in wait. They seemed to have a preference for men as all I got from them was hassle and cackle.

Avoiding the geese became something of a game for Shannon. She would turn and run in the opposite direction when they were on the rampage, leading them on then disappearing as quickly as she could. They got very cross when they couldn't find her and there was much hissing and flapping of wings. One morning she came unstuck as she turned sharply to make her escape, and came nose to beak with a hen in the garden. The squeaking and shrieking had us running to see what was happening. Poor Shannon, she wouldn't hurt a fly and we couldn't understand the commotion. Just as we arrived on the scene, a brood of twelve fluffy yellow chicks emerged from the long grass. They could only have been a few hours old and Mum was obviously protecting her babies.

The week went on and we managed all our chores, despite Laurel and Hardy's interference. The weather began to improve and we could at last see the rolling Welsh hills – when we had time to sit in the garden.

The one thing we couldn't get used to was the early morning call we had every day from the half dozen resident cockerels. They started calling to each other at 5.00am, and when they were all in full cry the noise was incredible, and we knew that was the end of any more sleep.

We did give ourselves a little time off to visit the odd castle and walk Shannon in the beautiful countryside, and it was soon the end of the week. What's that they say about time flying when you're having fun?

Well, it had certainly been different.

13

NPA COURSE

"Something for you to read here" said my boss one day as I arrived at work. The something was the programme for The National Pharmaceutical Association Medicine Counter Assistants Training course. This was all very new, and it had been created to help Pharmacy Assistants learn more about the products they were selling and recommending, and to give them more confidence whilst improving their product knowledge. I was one of the first to do the course, a guinea pig if you like, and quite reluctant, I might add.

I thought of all sorts of excuses not to go on the course, the main one being that I would have to go to Withington Hospital– wherever that was. Anyway, nothing ventured I thought, so I decided to go for it. Before I knew it, the forms were signed and in the post.

A week later, armed with map and instructions, found me on the way to Withington Hospital. A vast old rambling building which I was sure I would never find my way around, and it was miles and miles from Delph! As I walked into the hospital reception area, I met two more girls clutching the same instructions as me and looking equally lost. These were Maureen and Lesley, and along with Janet and Janice, we all became friends doing the course together and exchanging addresses and phone numbers when the course had finished.

None of us knew what to expect, so it was with some trepidation that we all filed into the lecture room for that first session. We needn't have worried. Even though it was quite intense, it was made interesting, even fun, by our course tutor, Paul, himself a community pharmacist.

The main aim of the course was to encourage us to ask our customers the right questions so that we could obtain as much information as possible, enabling us to make a correct sale, or refer to our pharmacist. An easy way to remember useful questions was *2WHAM*:

Who is it for?

What are the symptoms?

How long have they had the symptoms?

Actions already taken:

Medicines being taken:

We soon had this off by heart, and we were amazed how easy it was to put into practice back at our pharmacies.

Each session included group case studies where one of us would be the customer with a particular problem, and the rest of the group had to ask the correct questions. Well, what a laugh, you've never seen such acting, we should all have been on the stage.

As the course progressed, we all became more confident and knowledgeable. We covered all the day to day topics we were asked about regularly at work, such as indigestion and heartburn, constipation and diarrhoea, headaches and hay fever. We all agreed that we had a much better understanding of the products we were selling and consequently found our jobs more interesting.

The weeks flew by. It was the run-up to Christmas and we were all busy at work and at home, and it was sometimes a rush to have our homework done then travel to Withington. The last session was just before Christmas, so we decided to celebrate finishing the course with a bit of a party. We all took goodies and enjoyed chatting to each other on the last night and said how much we had enjoyed doing it. The course was described as intensive, and it was certainly that, but it had been good to meet girls from other pharmacies and make new friends. We all agreed it had been well worth doing.

And now I know where Withington is!

14

WINDOW DRESSING

Whenever I went on a Marketing and Display course, I remember being told that an interesting window display helps to encourage people to come into the shop. If the window is boring, the chances are that they will think it's not worth going in, so the answer is to come up with some original ideas if you can.

I really enjoyed doing the window displays. Being a former dental nurse, I was always interested in oral hygiene. My dentist was very helpful, and he let me borrow some instruments and other complementary items, including teeth which had recently been extracted. This made a really interesting, if a little gory, display, and it created a lot of interest. You could see people looking in the window with quite horrified expressions. I'm not sure if this actually encouraged customers to come into the shop or put them off altogether, but it was good fun doing it and watching their reactions.

The autumn window was always my favourite. The colours at that time of year are glorious, and there are so many different materials and props which can be used – most of them having nothing at all to do with selling pharmacy items. We've borrowed owls and squirrels from the local visitor centre. Not real ones, of course, but they were very life-like. Unfortunately, we couldn't quite accommodate a full-size badger and a fox. We've filled the window with heather cut straight from the surrounding moors, horse chestnuts and pine cones and bright red rose hips. A quick spray with hair lacquer helps to keep them shiny whilst they are in the window.

Amongst all this flora and fauna, I often had to be reminded that we did, in fact, need to put some pharmacy type stock in as well, as the general idea was to encourage sales, so a few health foods and vitamins were allowed in as well. The customers, as always in Delph, were very forthcoming with their comments. They were very good at standing outside the window when we were being creative and telling us just how it should be done. We didn't mind, it was all part of being involved with the community, and we usually thanked them for their input!

Sometimes, a company selling a certain product, perhaps hair colour, would have a competition and they wanted a creative window display showing their products to their best advantage. We enjoyed the challenge of entering these competitions. The prizes were often very good and you could win anything from hairdryers to holidays. It made the extra effort worthwhile when we won, which we were lucky enough to do quite a few times.

15

A SADDLEWORTH WINTER

The church clock was striking 3.00am and we were woken up by a sharp yapping from the garden below. Rubbing the sleep from our eyes, we looked out of the bedroom window to see a large dog-fox wandering around the lawn, his rusty coat shining in the moonlight. We watched him for a few minutes as he hunted around the garden in the hope of finding some juicy morsel abandoned by Shelley, our golden retriever. He was out of luck, nothing remotely edible ever escapes Shelley. Then he was off, across the field, no doubt back to his family in the hills beyond. How privileged we felt to have watched him there in our garden and not for the first time did we consider ourselves lucky to live here on the edge of the moor in this windswept corner of the Pennines.

Our house was built in the 1820s and part of it was once used as a small cotton mill. During the eighteenth and nineteenth centuries this area was full of home industries in the farmsteads and cottages scattered across the hillsides. Saddleworth farmers often supplemented their income by weaving, and it's not difficult to imagine how hard life would have been then. Winters were long and hard and homes could be cut off for weeks – no snow ploughs or gritters then just sheer hard work trying to dig yourself out.

Our small village is probably the most isolated of all the Saddleworth villages. It stands at around 1,000 feet above sea level and is only two miles from where the M62 motorway reaches its highest point as it crosses the Pennines. Part of the Pennine Way is also close by.

Our winters can be quite dramatic. Even with modern machinery to keep the roads clear, it doesn't take long for deep snow to accumulate when it blows off the moors, very quickly blocking the roads. It can be quite entertaining when car drivers choose to ignore 'Road Closed' signs thinking they can get through. The only thing to do is come back down the hill – backwards!

Saddleworth has a charm all of its own. Not really pretty like villages in the Cotswolds, but there is a toughness and solidity about it. Whenever you have been away, no matter how much you have enjoyed it, somehow you are always very glad to be back home.

Many chronicles have been written by local writers about life here in the past, and one particular story brings home how hard it must have been for working people living in the remote farms and cottages on the unforgiving moors.

One writer tells how, when he was a little boy, there was a great snowstorm which came in the middle of December. The lanes and tracks were filled with snow to the tops of the stone walls and huge drifts were piled up to the doors and windows of his house. The family ran out of paraffin for their lamps and they had very little coal. Christmas Eve arrived and they still couldn't get out. They huddled around the dying embers of the fire, using up all the coal they had left. Their Christmas dinner on that freezing cold day was a bowl of porridge and a spoonful of treacle.

Because there was very little coal in this area to fuel the mill engines, and it was never easy to transport goods, Saddleworth's Industrial development came to an end in the middle of the nineteenth century, which as far as today's residents and visitors are concerned, was no bad thing.

The Saddleworth year is full of lively events, many of them traditions, which have been carried on down the generations from those hard days of the past, and are now very much a tourist attraction bringing people from all over the country to share our special area. One quite spectacular event which takes place every August is The Longwood Thump Rushcart Festival. This custom dates back to medieval times when all the churches in the area covered their floors with rushes to keep the feet of the congregation warm and dry.

Nowadays, it's a gathering of Morris Men from all over the country, who come to take part in the festival. An enormous cart is built of rushes and one of the Morris Men has the dubious honour of sitting precariously on the top of the cart, while the rest of the team pull it around the villages. What a task!

They stop and dance in each village then the cart is taken up to the church, which is a very long and hard uphill pull, for the 'Blessing of the Rushes' service. It's an amazing sight to see. Hundreds of Morris Men in all their colourful finery, pulling a great cart made of rushes, with a man sitting on the very top. It really does have to be seen to be believed!

So, it's quite a special, if unusual place to live. Our hills may often be rain-lashed and grey, but when the sun shines on the heather, there's nowhere quite like it.

16

FIELDS OF CALENDULA

Barbara, my friend from work, and I were having a day out. We were not quite lost, just a bit lost – nothing that turning the map upside down wouldn't put right. I think most women read a map this way, and it seems perfectly logical to me.

We were on our way to an Open Day at the Weleda premises at Ilkeston, Derbyshire, where all the plants are grown for their homeopathic products. Derbyshire is where I'm from and I still think of it as home, so I didn't need much persuading to spend a day in that lovely part of the country, providing we could find our way there.

During recent years there has been a lot of interest in alternative and complementary medicine as more people turn to the natural approach to healthcare. We were beginning to sell quite a few products in this range as our customers became interested in the homeopathic side of medicine.

Back on course with the map now the right way round, we arrived in good time at a field dotted with marquees. Over coffee and delicious cake – always welcome – we looked through the list of activities and picked out the ones we thought would be interesting to us. We learnt that the products made there were based on the belief that humans thrive best when they use natural substances with which they have a natural affinity. This was our opportunity to see how these products were made and how they were intended to be used.

We had a busy schedule. There was so much to do and we wanted to do as much as possible. Our first stop was the 'Look and feel good' marquee which seemed a good place to start. Here we were offered a hand and foot massage. I wasn't quite sure about having my feet massaged, I thought it would be like having your feet tickled, but it was actually just wonderfully relaxing. Our feet were placed in a bowl of citrus milk which helps revitalise, then massaged with rose oil, skin food and foot balm. Just what we could do with after a day on our feet at the shop!

The flower fields were a sea of glorious colour, particularly the marigolds or to give them their proper name, calendula. We were able to collect some and see them go through each stage of preparation from chopping, weighing and liquidising to eventually being made into an ointment. Calendula is said to be good for treating cuts and as a general antiseptic for cleansing and disinfecting wounds.

We had a tour of the dispensary which was a wonderland of strange-sounding names, so different from the names on the products in our own dispensaries.

The day flew by, helped by more coffee and cake and other goodies. We treated ourselves to some of the soothing foot balm we had tried earlier. We left the golden calendula fields and set off on our journey home – without using the map, upside down or otherwise.

We felt we had learnt quite a lot about the alternative

approach to medicine. The principle of humans living in harmony with nature can only be a good thing and something we all strive for, though not always successfully.

17

TREACLE MINING

D eep in the heart of the Lancashire countryside lies a wealth of legend and history. Tales of witchcraft and folklore weave their spell to set the imagination racing amongst villages with names such as Sabden, Mitton and Langho.

Casting its gloomy shadow over these villages is Pendle Hill. It was here in the valley below where the tale of the Witches of Pendle began.

In the early 1600s, there lived two rival peasant families on the slopes of the hill. Both families were led by old women. One was called Demdyke, the other Chattox, and they were well-known in the area for roaming around the countryside, begging. Anyone who refused to give was immediately cursed and many strange and morbid things happened to them. Demdyke and Chattox, along with eighteen others who were also said to possess supernatural powers, were arrested and sent for trial. They were found guilty of witchcraft and finished up on the gallows on August 20th 1612. Even today, the very mention of Pendle Hill conjures up images of witches, and there still seems to be a spooky air hanging over it.

On a sunny Saturday, with friends who were staying the weekend, we packed a picnic and set off on the trail of the Pendle Witches. Little did we know that the highlight of our day was to be something far removed from sorcery and witchcraft.

We drove through the hills where Demdyke and Chattox had cast their spells. We became so involved, one of us reading the story out loud as we went, that we wouldn't have been at all surprised to see a broomstick fly past.

And then we saw the signpost!

We stopped, reversed the car and had another look just to make sure our eyes were not playing tricks on us, but there it was, quite clearly,

'To the Treacle Mines'

We couldn't resist it.

Following the directions, we soon came upon the cave–like entrance to the mines, not very sure what we were going to find. There was a guide to meet us, and we, along with Shannon our golden retriever, were welcomed to the Treacle Mines. We still couldn't quite believe we were doing this, as he began by telling us that the mines were the home of the Pendle Little People, whose ancestors had been able to stop the Romans invading their village by spreading treacle on the ground in front of their chariots.

We didn't dare look at each other. We found ourselves nodding sagely, how should we react, dare we laugh, no better not, our guide was very serious as he told his story to us. On we went, deeper into the mines. We were introduced to Uncle Silas Mitton, the present owner. He had reopened the mines after finding a small brown furry creature when he was out walking one day which turned out to be a treacle-eating boggart! He followed the little creature and noticed the ground he was walking on was very sticky and realised he had stumbled across an old treacle mine entrance.

We met Digger Calder and Willy Wizzle, two of the miners who had helped Silas reopen the Mine. Willy was especially clever and was given the post of chief treacle sniffer because of his amazing sense of smell. Nick O'Pendle, the village policeman and Preston Polly, the school teacher, were also there along with twins, Oswald and Twistle, who had a very special job. They were in charge of the black pudding trees which grew in front of the mine. The puddings had to be steamed in the Fog Factory and then bent into the familiar horseshoe shape – a very important job!

There was Ike Newton who had built a ginger beer pumping station at the head of the mine and piped the ginger beer down to the Parkin Cake Parlour below, where treacle toffee and parkin cake were made. An Irish Leprechaun called Brendan was in charge of bottling the beer. But because he was so homesick, he drank most it of whilst singing mournful Irish songs.

And so it went on, we gave up trying not to laugh. Was this really happening, we were in another world, and by the time we eventually emerged into the tiny shop where you could buy the delicious treacle toffee and ginger beer, we were thoroughly helpless and Shannon was very confused.

Still laughing, we left the treacle mines and the little people behind and headed for home. It had certainly been a day of contrasts, from looking for witches and finding treacle boggarts, but the question was, would anyone believe us when we told them about our day out down the mines?

We couldn't quite believe it ourselves, but perhaps the little brown furry creature with sticky paws that had found its way into the car, convinced us that it really had happened.

Footnote: *Tenuous Pharmacy connection.*

Apparently, the legend of the treacle mines originated in coal mining areas where tar deposits were washed into nearby streams. These lumps of tar were treacly in consistency and were melted down and dissolved in water to make a kind of disinfectant solution which was used to treat cuts and grazes. It was also considered useful for eye infections such as conjunctivitis.

Imagine being able to buy Treacle Eye Drops over the counter!

Second Footnote:

You may have seen Uncle Silas, Oswald and Twistle on television, as, sometime after our visit, a cartoon series was made about them and their adventures in the Treacle Mines.

18

A DAY AT PHARMACY HQ

You know what it's like when you have to be up at a certain time for a special reason, like going on holiday or having a day out. You can't be late, so you set the alarm incredibly early, wake up ages before it's due to go off, and when it jangles in your ear, all you want to do is turn over and go back to sleep.

I'd been invited to go to the presentation lunch for the Pharmacy Assistant of the Year, at Pharmacy headquarters in London. Very exciting, I was really looking forward to it. Barry, my husband, was coming along too, so the alarm was set for 5.30am.

I dragged myself from under the duvet with as much enthusiasm as is possible at that time in the morning. Our train wasn't due until 7.30am, but there were lots of things to do before we set off.

Luckily, a good friend was going to muck out Billy horse for me, so that was one thing less. However, Shannon, our golden retriever, who knew something different was going on, was to spend the day with Dad, where she would have a wonderful time being thoroughly spoilt. So it was on with the wellies to make sure she had a good walk before we dropped her off.

The train was on time and arrived at Euston Station at 10.00am, which gave us plenty of time to look around before making our way to Pharmaceutical H.Q. for lunch. We headed to Covent Garden and wandered through the colourful stalls and shops, some of them just opening, we were so early. We were able to pop into the newly refurbished Opera House and have a quick look. Being interested in opera and classical music in general, I would have liked to linger amongst the CDs and books in the shop, but we had to move on, time was going fast and we couldn't be late for lunch!

It was such a lovely sunny day, so we walked along Whitehall and we were just in time to see the changing of the guard. What superb horses. (Cover your ears, Billy). We could see the London Eye and made a note to take a trip on it some other time, it looked really good fun. On past Downing Street and the Palace of Westminster and we were soon crossing the river to Lambeth and our destination. We just had time for a quick look in the Museum of Garden History, which was fascinating. I bought some seeds to plant when I got back home, hoping they would survive in the wilds of Saddleworth.

We arrived for the presentation ceremony and heard that the three finalists all had the same marks and there was to be a tie-break for first place. Nail-biting stuff, glad it wasn't me, it must have been really nerve-racking for the girls involved. Eventually a decision was made and we all waited eagerly to hear the result. It was like being at the film awards. The president of the Pharmaceutical Society opened a gold envelope and announced: "The Pharmacy Assistant of the Year is.........". We held our breath, Sarah Williams. Much applause as Sarah was presented with a beautiful Caithness glass bowl and a £2,000 holiday voucher. There was another presentation to The Pharmacy

Interact Assistant of the Year, which is a different way of learning and taking part in the competition. We were all thrilled and excited for the winners and watched as they were photographed with their awards.

Then I had a surprise.

The Editor of the Pharmaceutical Journal, Doug Simpson, announced that there was to be another award, but the recipient didn't know anything about it.

It was me!

I was truly amazed. I had been writing for the publication 'The Pharmacy Assistant' for ten years and this was a special thank you. I was taken completely by surprise. It was one of those occasions when you wish something witty would pop into your head. But it didn't. I just hope I remembered to say 'Thank you, especially to Mr Simpson, as without his encouragement I may well have never written a word'. I walked back to my seat in a daze, clutching a heavy package.

I listened to the speakers telling us how important our role in the pharmacy is and how it will become even more important in the future as pharmacies take on more roles in healthcare. Training and knowledge were paramount so that we could advise our customers with confidence. I felt very proud to be there with the people who are at the front of our profession, who are interested in what we do and give us a great deal of support. It makes it all worthwhile.

After all the excitement, we were then able to chat over an excellent lunch and get to know each other as we talked about the different pharmacies we worked in. When we had finished lunch, there was another treat for us when we were given the opportunity to look around the building. We were shown the Council Chamber where major decisions were made and then we were able to see the museum, which was really interesting with all the ancient dispensing equipment. There were beautiful eye baths, apothecary jars with their Latin inscriptions, medicines and adverts from a bygone age. It was fascinating and we could have spent a long time there.

All too soon, it was time to leave. Yet another surprise awaited us. As we said 'goodbye and thanked everyone for a wonderful day, the winners and I were given bouquets of flowers. We stepped outside into the afternoon sunshine, clutching our flowers and feeling very special, after a day which I would certainly never forget.

Oh, and that heavy package? It was a beautifully illustrated book featuring just about every opera ever written, which I will treasure for always.

19

LIFE AFTER PHARMACY

When retired friends remarked that they didn't know how they had found time to go to work, I used to laugh and think what a ridiculous thing to say. Now, having joined the ranks myself, I know what they mean. I soon discovered that there was always something to do and my time was easily filled, mostly with longer and more frequent dog walks I have to admit.

After Tessa died, we approached Golden Retriever Rescue, as we thought we could help a dog in need of a good home. We knew we would have another dog, a friend for Leah who missed Tessa as much as we did, and we also knew that whoever came to us would have very big paws to fill. To follow in Tessa's footsteps was such a big act to follow. We were very lucky that day when we rang, as Holly's owners had also just rung to ask for help in finding another home for Holly.

Her owners were moving into a flat for health reasons, and although they could have taken her with them, there wasn't any garden or ground for her to run and play in. They were very brave to let her go, I couldn't have done it. She came straight to us without going to the rescue centre which of course was much better and, at just three years old, she was the perfect age to come and live with Leah. Confused at first – "Why am I here, where is my other Mum?" How do you explain? We just gave her lots of love and walks with Leah and she has settled into our routine, and now they are good friends.

So now we have another team – Leah and Holly - who happily take up most of our time and give us so much pleasure.

'The girls' as we call them, attract a lot of attention when we are out and about. Holly is everyone's friend and loves all the fuss, wagging her whole body from nose to tail. Leah is a bit more reserved but joins in not wanting to be left out.

Having dogs means that you have to go out whatever the weather. On cold, clear days in winter with the sun shining on the snow, the views from the tops of the hills can be spectacular and you are glad you made the effort, even when the roaring fire back at home seemed a much more inviting option. In summer it's just lovely to walk amongst the wild flowers in the valley below .

We are so lucky to have all this on our doorstep and to be part of this beautiful area with its own traditions, many of which are unique to Saddleworth.

Our own local Saddleworth poet, Ammon Wrigley, sums it up perfectly:

'Like the wind among the heather,
Just as careless and as free,
Up and down this old moor parish,
Let's go tramping, you and me.'

ABOUT THE AUTHOR

Margaret Ulyatt was born in Chesterfield, Derbyshire, where she still has family and many good friends. She moved over the Pennines to the hills of Saddleworth with her husband Barry when he started working in Manchester.

Margaret worked at the Pharmacy in the village of Delph, initially she thought, just for a short time. She stayed for 33 years. During that time she wrote many articles for the NPA magazine, The Pharmacy Assistant, about working in a rural pharmacy and life in a small village community. It is these articles that have prompted the writing of this book.

When she lived in Chesterfield she was a member of the Chesterfield Philharmonic Choir and Robinsons Operatic Society. She now sings with Saddleworth Musical Society and Oldham Choral Society.

She enjoys walking her two golden retrievers, Leah and Holly, and considers herself to be very lucky to be part of the very special area of Saddleworth.